CARING FOR CHEETAHS

MY AFRICAN ADVENTURE

ROSANNA HANSEN

BOYDS MILLS PRESS

Honesdale, Pennsylvania

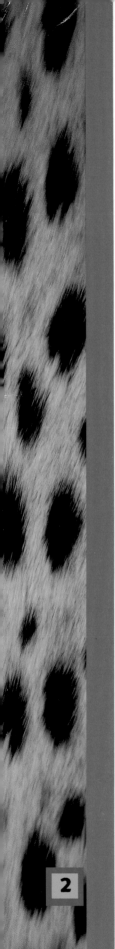

Photographs by Rosanna Hansen and
courtesy of the Cheetah Conservation
Fund with
supplemental photographs
as credited. See page 32.

Boyds Mills Press, Inc.
815 Church Street
Honesdale, Pennsylvania 18431
Printed in the United States of America

Book design by
R studio T, New York City

Supplemental photo research
by Julie Alissi

ACKNOWLEDGMENTS

Many thanks to everyone at CCF and
especially to Dr. Laurie Marker, Jen Newlin Bell,
Bonnie and Mandy Schumann,
Patricia Tricorache, Judith Walls,
Andrew Stein, and Dave Bell.
Their knowledge, help, and friendship have been
invaluable in researching, writing, and preparing the
photos for this book.

Special thanks also go to George Frame for his
careful review of the manuscript;
to my husband, Corwith Hansen, for being so
supportive of my cheetah research in Africa;
and to the cheetahs for always being
a source of inspiration.

A portion of the proceeds of this book
will be donated to the
Cheetah Conservation Fund's programs.

Library of Congress Cataloging-in-Publication Data
Hansen, Rosanna.
Caring for cheetahs : my African adventure / Rosanna Hansen
p. cm.
ISBN 978-1-59078-387-0 (hc) • ISBN 978-1-59078-825-7 (pb)
1. Cheetah—Namibia—Juvenile literature. 2. Hansen, Rosanna—
Juvenile literature. I. Title.

QL737.C23H3554 2007
599.75'9—dc22
2006018240

First edition
First Boyds Mills Press paperback edition, 2010
The text of this book is set in Adobe Garamond, Univers, and Advert Rough.

10 9 8 7 6 5 4 3 2 1 (hc)
10 9 8 7 6 5 4 3 2 1 (pb)

For Chewbaaka, Ralph, Sandy, Kanini,
and all the cheetahs CCF has helped.
Also for
Jen, Jan, and Linda,
who love cats big and small
as much as I do

—R.H.

▲ CCF's research and education center is in north-central Namibia, as shown on the map on page 13.

Yes, the cheetah you see on this page is real, and yes, I'm standing right beside him. The cheetah's name is Chewbaaka. He lives at a special nature reserve for cheetahs in Namibia, Africa. When this picture was taken, I worked at the nature reserve, caring for Chewbaaka and twenty-six other cheetahs. Chewbaaka's nature reserve is owned by the Cheetah Conservation Fund, or CCF. This group works to help cheetahs survive.

At CCF, I helped feed and care for orphaned cheetahs who live at the reserve. I also helped rescue an injured cheetah cub from the wild. The injured cub received medical care and a safe place to heal at CCF. And best of all, I had a chance to learn all about these beautiful big cats.

CHEWBAAKA'S "PLAY TREE"

When these photos were taken, Chewbaaka and I were visiting his favorite "play tree." Cheetahs use these special trees with sloping branches as scent posts.

As soon as he saw the tree, Chewbaaka headed straight for it. He paused to spray his scent on the trunk. Next, he jumped onto a branch and sniffed the scent of wild cheetahs who had passed by. After sniffing, Chewbaaka deposited some droppings to tell other cheetahs he had been there. Then he relaxed, looking out over the plains from his perch high in the tree.

In Namibia, these scent trees are called play trees or "newspaper trees." Cheetahs get the local news from the trees, finding out who has been there.

Chewbaaka sniffed the branch for a long time, finding out who had been there. When he was done, he relaxed and looked out over the plains.

DR. LAURIE AND CHEWBAAKA

My first day at CCF, I met Dr. Laurie Marker. Dr. Laurie is trained as a wildlife biologist and earned her Ph.D. degree studying cheetahs. She has worked with cheetahs for more than thirty years. Dr. Laurie founded CCF in 1990 to help cheetahs survive. As we talked, Laurie brought Chewbaaka out to meet me. Chewbaaka was calm, but I was nervous at first. Then Chewbaaka started to purr. He sounded like a great big house cat. After that, I calmed down. I even gave Chewbaaka some water and stroked his fur. Dr. Laurie said I could call Chewbaaka by his nickname, Mr. C.

When Chewbaaka was a tiny cub, he was orphaned. Without his mother, he would soon have starved or been eaten by a larger animal. Luckily, Chewbaaka was rescued and came to live at CCF when he was only three weeks old. Dr. Laurie fed him every day and cared for him while he grew up. Because Dr. Laurie raised Chewbaaka from the time he was tiny, he has bonded with her and sees her as part of his family.

Chewbaaka is relaxed and friendly with the staff and volunteers who help care for him. He even acts calm with people he's met for the first time—such as me.

▲ Dr. Laurie with Chewbaaka, who is standing with his front paws on a termite mound. Cheetahs often climb large termite mounds to look over the surrounding countryside.

ROYAL COMPANIONS

Not all kinds of animals can be tamed, but cheetahs have a long history of living with people as pets. For centuries, cheetahs were the tame hunting companions of kings and princes in Egypt and India. Why were cheetahs chosen to live with royalty? Because cheetahs are much less aggressive than other big cats such as lions, tigers, and leopards. (When a cheetah sees one of these other big cats, the cheetah runs away.) Also, cheetahs are more social than tigers or leopards.

Some people used to keep cheetahs as pets in the United States. But since 1973, when the U.S. Endangered Species Act was passed, only zoos and wildlife parks have been allowed to keep cheetahs. The Endangered Species Act helps to protect cheetahs and other animals that are in danger of extinction.

Today, Chewbaaka works as an ambassador for cheetahs. He helps Dr. Laurie teach groups that visit CCF about cheetahs and what people can do to help them.

Because he was hand-reared by Dr. Laurie, Chewbaaka is at ease with people. He doesn't mind if humans come near him or sometimes even touch him.

▲ Chewbaaka likes to lap up water from a big wooden spoon—and I loved to hold the spoon for him. In the background, you can see Chewbaaka's favorite "play tree."

MEETING MORE CHEETAHS

After I met Dr. Laurie and Chewbaaka, I toured the CCF reserve and met the twenty-six other cheetahs. I was surprised to see how different they were. Some were young, playful cubs; others were old and cranky. Some were curious, while others were quiet and shy.

These CCF cheetahs had many differences, but they were all alike in one way: none of them acted as calm around people as Chewbaaka did. These other CCF cheetahs are not tame like Chewbaaka, but rather are habituated to humans. By living near humans and being fed by them regularly, these CCF cheetahs have become used to people. A habituated cheetah can tolerate a person's presence better than a wild cheetah can. But habituated cheetahs are not tame like house pets, either. They can still be unpredictable and sometimes even dangerous.

Most of the cheetahs who live at the reserve had been hurt or orphaned when they were young. They couldn't live on their own, so CCF rescued them and gave them a safe home.

◄ This adult male cheetah lived in a large pen close to my hut. I took pictures of him every morning before breakfast.

The CCF cheetahs live in big, open pens with lots of room to run and play. In fact, some of the pens are so big that the CCF workers can't always find the cheetahs right away. If the cheetahs are nowhere to be seen, workers bringing food to them call out, "C'mon, c'mon—come, come, come!" Then the cheetahs usually come running.

At CCF, some of the cheetah pens are so big that you can't see the fences on the far side.

Once I had met all the cheetahs, I got settled into my rondavel (a round hut with a roof made of reeds or sticks). That's the kind of house many Africans live in. I shared my hut with tiny lizards called geckos and many birds that nested in the roof. The geckos didn't bother me, but the birds started singing at dawn. They were much louder than an alarm clock.

FEEDING THE CHEETAHS

▲ My rondavel at CCF.

The day after I moved in, I started work. My most important job was helping to feed all the cheetahs. These big cats need a diet of meat to stay healthy. Each day, we filled twenty-seven food dishes with chunks of meat. We added a little calcium and some vitamins to the meat, too. Then we took the meat dishes to the cheetahs' pens—and usually walked right in. At first I was scared. But I soon found that the cheetahs left us alone. They were more interested in the food than in us.

When we went into the pens, we worked in pairs. One person carried the food. The other carried a long stick, just in case a cheetah got scared or upset. We talked to the cheetahs calmly to reassure them as we set down the food dishes. Once we stepped away, the cheetahs would rush over to the food. Then we could clean up other parts of the pens while all the cheetahs were busy eating.

CHEETAHS THEN AND NOW

More than 100,000 cheetahs once lived in Africa and Asia. But over the past hundred years, the number of cheetahs in the world has fallen close to extinction. Over the years, hunters and farmers killed many cheetahs across their entire range. People also destroyed much of the cheetahs' habitat, turning grasslands into farms and ranches.

Scientists now estimate that only about 12,000 cheetahs are left in the wild, mostly in southern and eastern Africa. About 3,000 of these cheetahs live in Namibia—more than in any other country.

Two of the cheetahs we fed were big, strong males who weren't well habituated to humans. We didn't go inside their pen. Instead, we set out food for them in a special small cage. Then we left the cage and let the big male cheetahs in so they could eat.

▲ When the cheetahs heard us calling, they usually came running to get their food.

As mentioned before, cheetahs are not as large or fierce as lions or tigers. So it was safe to go in all but one of the cheetah pens with just a long stick to protect us. Once in a while, a young cheetah got upset and hissed or growled. Those sounds meant the young cheetah was scared and defensive, so we moved extra slowly and spoke calmly. When we put down the food and backed away, the cheetah would relax and eat its food. We never had to use the stick to keep a cheetah from coming too close during my stay at the reserve.

It was always fun to bring the cheetahs food and see how beautiful they are. I especially loved to watch the cheetahs playing together or grooming one another after they had eaten their dinner.

▲ This nervous cub tipped over his food bowl as he backed away from us.

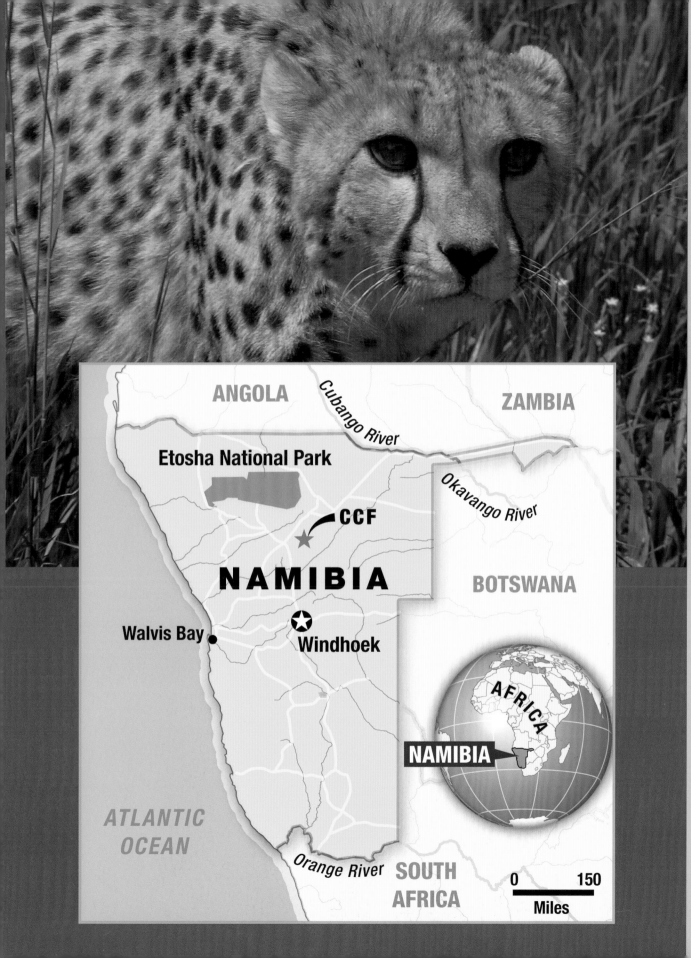

NAMIBIA: CHEETAH CAPITAL OF THE WORLD

Namibia is a country in southwestern Africa. The dry inland part is desert and high, rolling plains. The CCF research center and reserve is located in north-central Namibia, on the high plains. Many wild animals live in and around the CCF reserve. When we drove from CCF to the nearest town for supplies, we saw giraffes, antelopes, warthogs, zebras, and even an occasional wild cheetah. Namibia is often called the "cheetah capital of the world" because of the 3,000 wild cheetahs that live there.

About 120 miles north of the CCF reserve is Etosha National Park, one of the largest animal parks in Africa. If you wait at a water hole in Etosha for several hours, you can sometimes see hundreds of animals, all coming to drink.

Cheetahs are members of the cat family (Felidae) and graceful, like all cats. They have golden coats with black spots, and teardrop markings run from their eyes down to their mouths. When they are young, they have a ruff, or mantle, of long silver gray fur on their backs and shoulders.

Cheetahs are champion sprinters. In fact, they can run faster than any other land animal in the world. At top speed, a few cheetahs have been timed at a blistering 70 miles per hour. And lots of cheetahs can run 65 miles per hour. At either of those speeds, the cheetahs are running faster than horses or antelopes or any other speedy land animals. Also, cheetahs can go from standing still to top speeds in only about five seconds. Some sports cars can accelerate faster than a cheetah, but not many.

Every cheetah has slightly different markings on its face. We learned to identify each cheetah at CCF by the unique shape of its teardrop markings, the shape of its eyes, and the markings on its tail.

However, a cheetah can race at its top speed for only a few hundred yards. Then it gets out of breath, its body gets too hot, and the cheetah has to rest.

Like all big cats, cheetahs in the wild hunt for their food. They need their amazing speed and sharp eyesight to help them race after antelopes and other prey.

FAST CHEETAH FACTS

- **Adult size:** 80 to 140 pounds; 26 to 32 inches high at the shoulder
- **Lifespan:** 7 to 12 years in the wild; as long as 21 years in captivity (average age range in captivity: 7–15 years)
- **Family:** Felidae, or cat family
- **Scientific name:** *Acinonyx jubatus. Acinonyx* means "nonmoving claws." (Cheetahs don't fully retract their claws as other cats do.) And *jubatus* means "maned." (Young cheetahs have a mane, or mantle, of long silvery fur on their backs and shoulders.)

- **Status:** At risk of extinction: "endangered" under the U.S. Endangered Species Act; "vulnerable" according to the IUCN (The World Conservation Union) Red List of Threatened Species

This cheetah is standing on a termite mound, scanning the countryside.

HUNTING IN THE WILD

When a wild cheetah starts a hunt, it often climbs a tree or even a tall termite mound. From there, the cheetah scans the plains until it spots a likely target—a small antelope on the edge of its herd, perhaps. The cheetah starts to creep as close as possible to the antelope. Suddenly, the cheetah bursts out of its hiding place and races toward its prey. By the time the antelope leaps away in a panic, the cheetah has already closed in. If the cheetah catches the antelope, it will drag its prey to the ground and kill it. But the cheetah is successful in its hunts only about half the time. The rest of the time, the prey outlasts the cheetah and gets away, then the cheetah goes hungry.

Meat eaters like cheetahs are an important part of their ecosystems and food chains. By hunting the weak, sick, or slow members of an antelope herd, a cheetah helps to keep the herd healthy and strong. Also, cheetahs are partly responsible for maintaining a balance between the number of prey animals and the amount of plant food available for them to eat. Without predators like the cheetah, the herds of prey animals might get too large. When there are too many prey animals, there is not enough plant food to go around. Then the herd animals may get weak and start to starve.

▼ During a chase, both the antelope and cheetah run at top speed.

BUILT FOR THE CHASE

A cheetah's body is an elegant running machine. Cheetahs have:

- **A long, flexible spine**

The cheetah's backbone acts like a giant spring, coiling and uncoiling as the cheetah runs.

- **Long, thin legs and claws that grip firmly**

The cheetah's long, blunt claws act like the spikes on track shoes. The spikes keep the cheetah from skidding when it sprints.

- **A small, sleek head with large nostrils**

The cheetah's big nostrils help it inhale and exhale huge quantities of air while it runs, supplying its body with oxygen and getting rid of carbon dioxide.

- **Large eyes and keen eyesight**

The cheetah can see for long distances and detect tiny movements in the brush. Also, the black "teardrop" marks running down from a cheetah's eyes may reduce glare from the sun, like the black smudges that football players wear under their eyes.

- **A long, muscular tail**

A cheetah's tail acts like a counterweight, keeping the cheetah on course as it whips around curves at scorching speed.

RACE FOR SURVIVAL

Cheetahs are famous for their record-breaking speed as they race after their prey. But lately, the cheetahs' biggest race has been for survival. With only about 12,000 cheetahs left in the wild, scientists worry that these amazing creatures may die out completely unless people help them. In the 1980s alone, more than 7,000 cheetahs were killed in Namibia. Back then, Dr. Laurie was alarmed by how quickly the cheetahs were being killed. That's why she set up CCF in 1990 in north-central Namibia—the heart of cheetah country.

Today, CCF has a full-time staff at its Namibian research center and reserve. The staff members take part in scientific research, rescue

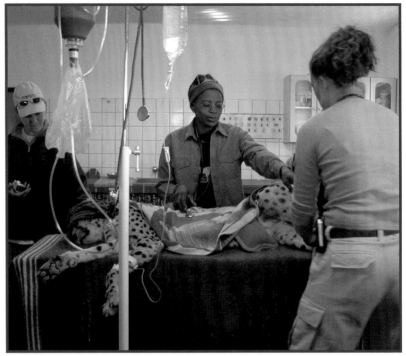

▲ CCF staffers can treat injured cheetahs in their own veterinary clinic.

This cheetah was badly injured in an illegal trap and later recovered.

injured cheetahs, oversee the care of CCF's resident big cats, and release some rescued cheetahs back into the wild. Volunteers and science students assist the staff members with their work. CCF now has branches in several other countries, including Canada, Kenya, the United Kingdom, and the United States.

CCF works closely with other African wildlife organizations that help cheetahs, such as Cheetah Outreach and the De Wildt Cheetah and Wildlife Conservation Centre. For more information about these organizations, see page 31.

DR. LAURIE'S HOPE FOR THE FUTURE

"Cheetahs need to be here in Namibia, living free in the wild. I hope that people can learn to live in peace with the cheetah, sharing this beautiful land and its resources. That's why our motto at CCF is 'We can live together.'

"Through CCF's programs, I believe that our dream can come true—that cheetahs can survive and live free, as they have for hundreds of thousands of years. To make that dream come true, CCF needs help. If enough people help, we can make sure the cheetah survives for future generations."

Dr. Laurie with Chewbaaka and Koya, an Anatolian shepherd dog

19

A DAY AT THE RACES

▲ First, we set up the racetrack motor in a grassy field.

My favorite job at CCF was cheetah racing. Cheetahs need to exercise to stay fit. To help them do that, we set up a special racetrack in a grassy field.

The cheetahs got excited when it was time to race. As we set up the track, they swished their tails and started to pace. When they ran, the cheetahs chased a cotton rag tied to a string. The string was pulled around the track by a small motor.

The first day I helped set up the racetrack, three young female cheetahs were racing. My favorite was a cheetah named Sandy. When everything was ready, we started the motor. *Whoosh*—the cheetahs took off. These young female cheetahs could sprint from 0 to more than 60 miles an hour in a few seconds.

The first cheetah flashed by me, her tail flying as she zoomed around the track. Suddenly, Sandy surged in front. Round the track the cheetahs raced, until Sandy dashed way ahead and snatched the cotton rag from the string. "Good girl, Sandy!" I told her. For a reward, she was given a small piece of meat.

Before they raced again, the cheetahs needed to rest for a while. They can sprint at top speed for only a few minutes before they have to rest. If the cheetahs don't stop and rest, their bodies might overheat. Overheating is serious—it could make the cheetahs sick or even kill them. So we let the cheetahs rest whenever they got too hot and tired. After resting, they would get up and seem eager to race again.

That day, Sandy won two races.

▲ Then, Sandy (left) and her sister Blondi took off at a blazing pace.

First she would pounce on the rag and yank it off the string. Then she'd look around for her tasty prize. As we hurried over to feed her, I decided that cheetah racing was the best job ever. When all three cheetahs finished racing that day, we let them have a long, lazy rest.

3 When cheetahs race at full speed, they use their long tails for balance.

▲ Sandy surged ahead, grabbing the rag on the string.

▲ The winner's prize: a tasty chunk of meat.

CHEETAH SOUNDS

Cheetahs do not roar like lions or tigers. To call one another, they often make birdlike chirping sounds. When they are upset or nervous, they hiss or growl. Cheetahs also make bleating sounds, similar to mewing, when they are unhappy. A mother cheetah sometimes calls her cubs with a special "stutter" call—or with a chirp. When cheetahs are happy and relaxed, they purr loudly.

▶These young cubs have long fur mantles on their backs and shoulders.

GROWING UP WILD

Male and female cheetahs may mate at any time of the year, and the female will give birth after about three months of pregnancy. A litter of newborn cheetahs usually includes three to four cubs.

When the cubs are born, they have long gray fur called a mantle on their backs and shoulders. Some scientists think this mantle may help the cubs hide in tall brush while their mother goes off to hunt. Lions, leopards, hyenas, and other large animals will kill cheetah cubs if they get the chance. To help protect her cubs, the mother cheetah will move them to a new hiding spot every few days. Still, many cheetah cubs are killed.

When the cubs are about six weeks old, they start to follow their mother and watch while she hunts. If the mother kills an animal, she will

A MALE HUNTING TEAM

When I visited Etosha National Park in northern Namibia, I saw two male cheetahs hunting together as a team. They were lucky the time I watched them— they killed an impala antelope and ate well that day. Scientists think that male cheetahs probably increase their chances of success when they hunt as a team.

▲ These cubs are old enough to go with their mother while she hunts. Soon they will learn to hunt for themselves.

make a special sound to call the cubs. She may chirp like a bird or make a strange "stutter" call. The cubs chirp back to her and come running for their dinner. First the cubs eat, and then it's the mother's turn. After dinner, they rest, groom one another, and usually purr together loudly. When the cubs get older, the mother teaches them how to hunt for themselves.

At about eighteen months of age, the cubs will leave their mother and go off to live as adults. Some of the cubs may stay together for a while, but the females will live alone with their cubs once they start having babies. Two or more of the brothers may stay together their whole lives and hunt in a group called a coalition.

CONFLICTS WITH FARMERS

Most of the wild cheetahs in Namibia live on farmland—not in animal reserves. That makes it easy for farmers to hunt and kill cheetahs. For many years, farmers would kill a cheetah whenever they saw one. The farmers thought cheetahs were killing and eating their cows or goats instead of eating wild game.

Scientists at CCF weren't sure that wild cheetahs really were eating farm animals. To find out, the scientists put radio collars on wild cheetahs and tracked them by airplane. For about ten years, the scientists studied wild cheetahs and their prey. The scientists proved the cheetahs almost always ate wild animals—not farm animals like cows and goats.

Now the CCF staffers work with farmers and tell them the truth about wild cheetahs. When farmers learn the facts, some of them agree not to kill any more cheetahs. Instead, the farmers promise to call CCF whenever they find an orphaned cub or a problem cheetah eating livestock. Then CCF workers can rescue the cheetah, check its health, and take it far away from the farm. That way, the farmer doesn't have to worry about the cheetah—and the cheetah stays alive.

Some of the rescued cheetahs stay at CCF because they are too young or weak to survive in the wild. But many rescued cheetahs are healthy, strong, and old enough to be released.

◀ The day a cheetah is released, CCF workers move the cat into a transport crate and drive into the bush.

▼ At the release site, a CCF manager lifts the sliding door of the crate—and the cheetah runs out to live free once more.

▲ This cheetah cub is too young to know how to hunt for itself. It can't be released to the wild. Instead, it will have a safe home and plenty of food at CCF.

Cheetahs that can be returned to the wild stay at CCF only for a few days—they mustn't become habituated to people and feel safe around them. If a cheetah were released after it became habituated, it might try to return to human company and would then become a problem. Also, a habituated cheetah loses its natural shyness, which is its best defense against hunters.

TO THE RESCUE

One day at CCF, I helped rescue an injured cheetah cub. Early Sunday morning, I was making tea in the volunteers' kitchen when the phone rang. The call was from a farmer, Ralph Ritter, who had found a wounded cheetah cub on his land. He said it had a broken leg that looked infected. Could we rescue it right away?

No time for breakfast! We loaded the truck, grabbed some snacks, and started on the long trip to the farm. Two hours later, we arrived. The poor little cub was trying to hide inside a big truck tire. We could see a nasty gash on the cub's front leg. And the cub looked thin, weak, and terrified.

With Ralph Ritter's help, we placed the cub into the rescue crate and loaded it into the van. Then we headed straight to the veterinarian's hospital. The vet took one look and said the cub needed surgery right away. He also asked us to help him perform the surgery. The vet had no staff on Sundays, and the surgery couldn't wait. *Gulp!*

First, we gave the cub a drug so it would sleep through the operation. Then I helped move the cub to the operating table. My job was to hand surgical instruments to the vet. The vet first had to clean the cub's broken leg and then cut the infection out of the bone. After that, he set the bone and put a cast on it.

I was afraid that I might get sick or faint during the operation, but I was fine. I just concentrated on helping the cub so that I wouldn't think about the blood and broken bone. And it felt great to help save a cheetah cub that would have died without us.

When we first saw the injured cub, he was hiding in a big truck tire.

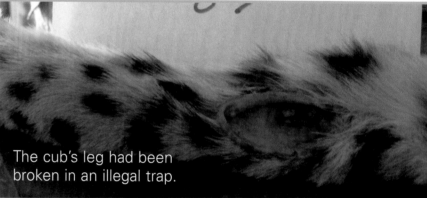

The cub's leg had been broken in an illegal trap.

We knew the cub was quite young because he still had a mantle of long fur on his shoulders.

After the surgery, the cub stayed with the vet for several days. When the cub's leg was better, the vet brought him to the CCF reserve. We were all excited to see the cub again, looking healthy this time. After a lot of discussion, we decided to name the cub Ralph, in honor of Ralph Ritter. Soon little Ralph learned how to walk and trot with a cast on his leg. Several weeks later, the cub's leg had healed completely. Then little Ralph could walk and run like all the other cheetahs.

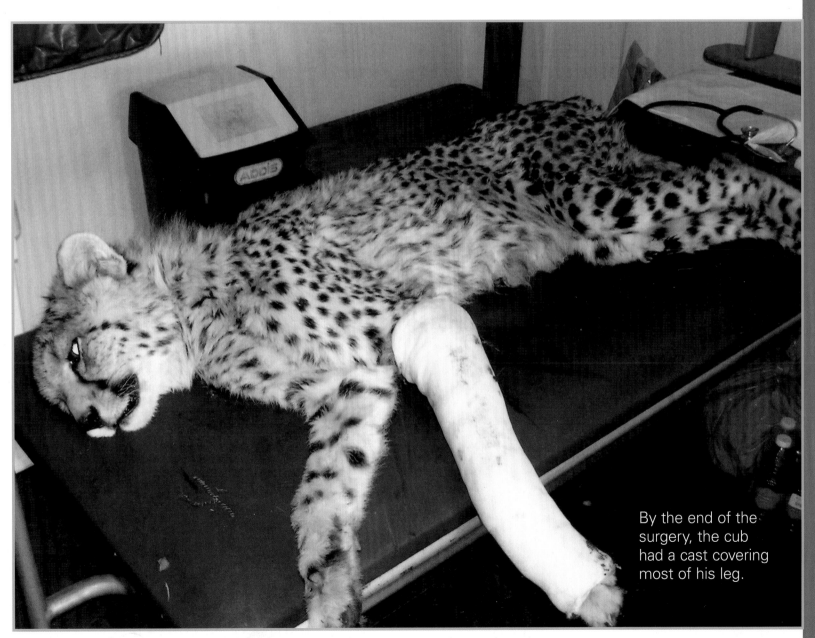

By the end of the surgery, the cub had a cast covering most of his leg.

GUARD DOGS AND GOATS

Besides removing cheetahs from farmland, CCF helps farmers in another way. They give farmers guard dogs for their goats and other livestock. The dogs are Anatolian shepherds, a special kind of guard dog from Turkey. CCF cares for the mother dogs and raises the young puppies with baby goats. When the puppies are old enough, CCF donates each puppy to a farmer. When the farmer gets the puppy, he puts it right in with his own goats. The puppy stays with the goats all day. Living this way helps the puppies bond with the goats and want to protect them.

Once the puppies grow up, they guard the goats out in the grasslands. If a wild cheetah comes too near the goats, the guard dog will bark and scare the cheetah away. Thanks to his guard dog, the farmer doesn't have to worry about cheetahs bothering his goats. That's how the guard dogs can help farmers and cheetahs live together in peace.

These Anatolian shepherd puppies have just been born.

◀ One of my jobs at CCF was helping to care for Chester, a male Anatolian shepherd.

When the puppies are a few weeks old, they will be raised with baby goats.

KIDS HELPING CHEETAHS

When schoolchildren visit CCF, they learn how to help these big cats survive. They can become "cheetah ambassadors" by telling their families and friends that cheetahs are endangered and need our help.

Kids in the United States help cheetahs, too. Some kids write articles or letters about the cheetah's plight for their school newspapers. A third-grade class in Fremont, California, raised money to pay for the care of several cheetahs.

To read more about how kids can help, go to www.cheetah.org and click on Kids4Cheetahs.

Dr. Laurie meets with a group of schoolchildren at CCF.

KIDS AND CHEETAHS, FACE-TO-FACE

Each year, hundreds of Namibian schoolchildren visit CCF's education center. I had fun meeting some of the students and helping to show them around. Most of them had never seen a cheetah before, so they laughed and talked with excitement. Then, when Chewbaaka and Dr. Laurie walked up to meet them, the students fell silent. For a minute, Chewbaaka's purring was the only sound. Then Dr. Laurie told the students about Chewbaaka and allowed some of them to pet his fur. After that, CCF staffers and volunteers taught the students about cheetahs.

WHY HELP THE CHEETAH?

Some people don't agree with CCF and its goals. These people ask me why I want to help cheetahs, anyway. Why work to save a few big cats? What's the point?

For me and for people at CCF, the answers are clear. We want to help cheetahs because:

- **Cheetahs are unique.** With their blazing speed, cheetahs are the fastest land animals on Earth.
- **Cheetahs help maintain the balance of nature,** removing old, slow, and sick animals from herds of prey animals.
- **Cheetahs are beautiful.** These big cats are among the world's most elegant, graceful creatures.
- **Cheetahs, like all animals, have a rightful place in the world.**

People have harmed cheetahs, hunting them almost to extinction. But now groups like CCF are helping them make a comeback. When Dr. Laurie started CCF in 1990, time was running out for cheetahs. No one knew how long these big cats could survive in the wild. Today, thanks to CCF and other wildlife groups, the cheetah's chances are improving. Farmers are learning to live peacefully with these elegant cats. And Namibia's cheetah population has slowed its decline. For the first time in years, there is hope that cheetahs may be able to survive.

My last week at CCF, I visited Etosha National Park. I was lucky—I saw some wild cheetahs there. As I watched them run and play, I thought about how special cheetahs are—and how much they need help. That's why CCF and groups like it are so important. Through their work, people can help protect cheetahs so their numbers don't decline. With our help, cheetahs can win their race for survival.

FOR MORE INFORMATION

If you would like to learn more about African wildlife groups that help cheetahs, here are some Web sites* for you to check:

Cheetah Conservation Fund (CCF)

CCF's Web site has a section called Kids4Cheetahs, which tells what kids can do to help the cheetah. The Web site also describes CCF's work in Namibia and Kenya and offers general information on all of its activities. www.cheetah.org

Cheetah Outreach

This South African conservation group works closely with CCF and with the De Wildt Cheetah and Wildlife Conservation Centre. www.cheetah.co.za

De Wildt Cheetah and Wildlife Conservation Centre

This South African wildlife center specializes in conservation and breeding programs for cheetahs and other endangered animals. www.dewildt.org.za

*Active at time of publication

GLOSSARY

coalition a group of male cheetahs that live together and form a hunting team

ecosystem a community of living things (animals, plants, etc.) that interact with one another and with their nonliving environment (soil, water, weather, etc.)

endangered refers to living things (animals, plants, etc.) that are in danger of becoming extinct

extinct describes a species of living things (animals, plants, etc.) that has died out completely and no longer exists

habituated used to or accustomed to something or someone

mantle a large patch of long fur on a cheetah cub's back and shoulders

predator an animal that hunts and kills other animals for its food (see *prey*)

prey an animal that is hunted and eaten by another animal (see *predator*)

retract to pull back

rondavel a round hut with a roof made of thatch (reeds, sticks, or grasses)

species a group of animals that breed with one another, giving birth to healthy young that can also breed successfully in adulthood

sprint to run as fast as possible for a short distance

PHOTO CREDITS

ABOUT THE AUTHOR

Rosanna Hansen has worked in children's books
as a publisher, an editor in chief, and an author.
Most recently, she served as publisher and editor in chief
of Weekly Reader, supervising seventeen classroom magazines
as well as books. Before that, she was group publisher of
Reader's Digest Children's Books.

Rosanna has written more than seventeen children's books
on such topics as animals, nature, and astronomy.
In her free time, she helps raise guide-dog puppies and
volunteers for wildlife organizations such as
the Cheetah Conservation Fund.

She and her husband, Corwith, live in Tuckahoe, New York.

INDEX